Ripley's PIRATES
Believe It or Not!®

TWISTS

RIPLEY
PUBLISHING

a Jim Pattison Company

Written by Camilla de la Bedoyere
Illustrations by John Graziano

RIPLEY
PUBLISHING

Executive Vice President, Intellectual Property Norm Deska
Vice President, Archives and Exhibits Edward Meyer
Director, Publishing Operations Amanda Joiner
Managing Editor Dean Miller

Editor Wendy A. Reynolds, M.S.Ed.
Designers Sam South, Joshua Surprenant
Researcher Sabrina Sieck
Additional Research Jessica Firpi
Fact Checker, Anglicisation James Proud
Production Coordinator Amy Webb
Reprographics Juice Creative Ltd
Cover Concept Joshua Surprenant
Cover Art John Graziano

www.ripleys.com/books

Copyright 2015 by Ripley Entertainment Inc.
First published in Great Britain by
Random House Books in 2015

Random House Books
20 Vauxhall Bridge Road
London SW1V 2SA
www.randomhouse.co.uk

Random House Books is part of the Penguin Random
House group of companies whose addresses can be found
at global.penguinrandomhouse.com

Penguin
Random House
UK

ISBN 978-1-78475-314-6

A CIP catalogue record for this book is available from
the British Library.

Manufactured in China in June 2015. First Printing.

WARNING: Some of the stunts and activities are undertaken by experts and
should not be attempted by anyone without adequate training and supervision.

CONTENTS

Pirates *of* the *World*

THE HAIR-RAISING TRUTH!

You're standing on the deck of a huge wooden ship. The smell of gunpowder is thick in the air. Everywhere you look men are fighting for their lives, and the clashing sound of swords and cutlasses is cut only by their screams. Your captain signals for you to join them – all for your share of the treasure that lies in the ship's hold. Do you have what it takes to be a pirate?

If you do, then prepare for an exciting pirate adventure! You'll learn lots of important pirate lingo, hints for designing your own pirate flag, and tips for creating your personal pirate "look". You'll also find unbelievable facts about some of the most famous pirates in history, including their evil raids, hidden treasures, and terrible ends.

Found a new word? Big Word Alert will explain it for you.

BIG WORD ALERT

— RIGGING —

The ropes and chains used to attach sails to the masts and yards.

When a petrified passenger refused to hand over a diamond ring, Blackbeard simply sliced off his finger!

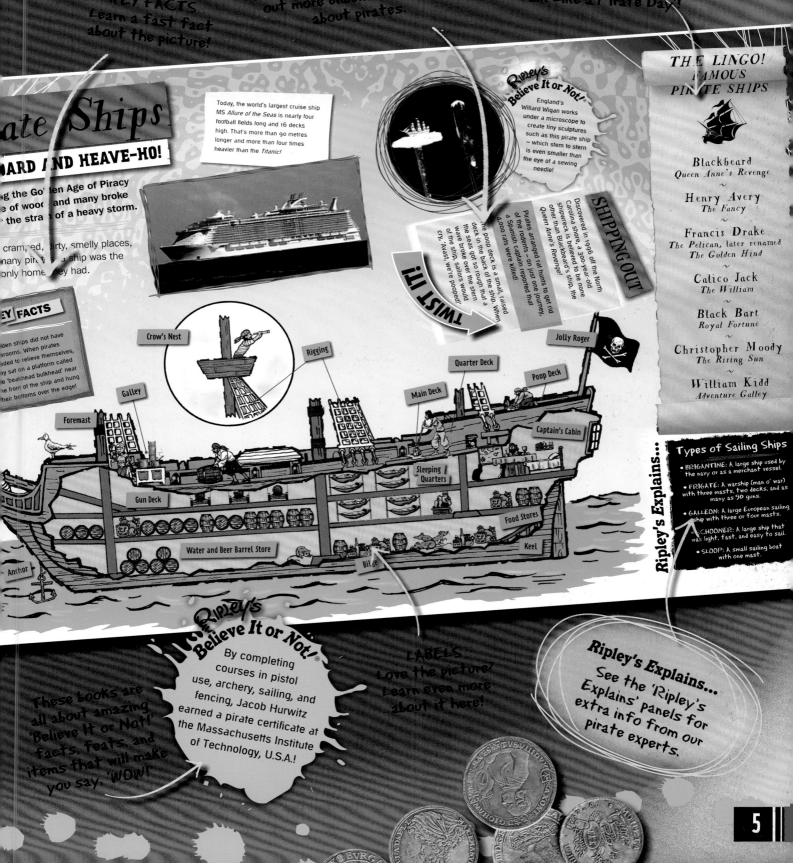

KEY FACTS
Learn a fast fact about the picture!

Don't forget to look out for the 'Twist It!' column on some pages. Twist the book to find out more unbelievable facts about pirates.

AAAARG! Practice the pirate lingo on the scrolls throughout this book and on September 19, you'll be ready to celebrate 'International Talk Like a Pirate Day'!

...ate Ships

...ARD AND HEAVE-HO!

...g the Golden Age of Piracy
...e of wood, and many broke
... the stra... of a heavy storm.

...cramped, dirty, smelly places,
...many pira... a ship was the
only home they had.

Today, the world's largest cruise ship MS *Allure of the Seas* is nearly four football fields long and 16 decks high. That's more than 90 metres longer and more than four times heavier than the *Titanic!*

Ripley's Believe It or Not!
England's Willard Wigan works under a microscope to create tiny sculptures such as this pirate ship – which stem to stern is even smaller than the eye of a sewing needle!

SHIPPING OUT

Discovered in 1926 off the North Carolina shore, a 300-year-old shipwreck is believed to be none other than Blackbeard's ship, the *Queen Anne's Revenge!*

Pirates arranged rat hunts to get rid of the rodents – on just one journey, a Spanish captain reported that 4,000 rats were killed!

TWIST IT!

The poop deck is a small, raised deck in the back of the ship. When the seas got so rough that a wave broke over the stern of the ship, sailors would cry, 'Avast, we're pooped!'

THE LINGO! FAMOUS PIRATE SHIPS

Blackbeard
Queen Anne's Revenge
~
Henry Avery
The Fancy
~
Francis Drake
The Pelican, later renamed
The Golden Hind
~
Calico Jack
The William
~
Black Bart
Royal Fortune
~
Christopher Moody
The Rising Sun
~
William Kidd
Adventure Galley

...EY FACTS
...den ships did not have
...rooms. When pirates
...ded to relieve themselves,
...ey sat on a platform called
...e 'beakhead bulkhead' near
...he front of the ship and hung
...heir bottoms over the edge!

Crow's Nest
Rigging
Galley
Foremast
Quarter Deck
Main Deck
Poop Deck
Jolly Roger
Captain's Cabin
Sleeping Quarters
Gun Deck
Food Stores
Water and Beer Barrel Store
Keel
...Anchor
Bilge

Ripley's Explains...

Types of Sailing Ships
• **BRIGANTINE:** A large ship used by the navy or as a merchant vessel.
• **FRIGATE:** A warship (man o' war) with three masts, two decks, and as many as 90 guns.
• **GALLEON:** A large European sailing ship with three or four masts.
• **SCHOONER:** A large ship that was light, fast, and easy to sail.
• **SLOOP:** A small sailing boat with one mast.

Ripley's Believe It or Not!
By completing courses in pistol use, archery, sailing, and fencing, Jacob Hurwitz earned a pirate certificate at the Massachusetts Institute of Technology, U.S.A.!

These books are all about amazing 'Believe It or Not!' facts, feats, and items that will make you say, 'WOW!'

LABELS
Love the picture? Learn even more about it here!

Ripley's Explains...
See the 'Ripley's Explains' panels for extra info from our pirate experts.

The Golden Age of Pirates

A TIMELINE OF TERROR...

Pirates have troubled sea travellers for many centuries. There was one brief time in history – the Golden Age of Piracy – when pirates actually controlled the seas.

From 1650 to 1730, fleets of pirate ships wreaked havoc around the Mediterranean Sea, across the Atlantic, in the China Sea and the Bay of Bengal, and throughout the Caribbean.

Pirate ship crews could range between two and 300 members.

The sloop was a popular choice for a pirate ship.

PIRATES' LOG BOOK:

Key Events in History

Ripley's Explains...

BCE

BCE is short for Before Common Era. If a date says 250 BCE, and the current year is 2016, add the two numbers to work out when the event happened: 2016 + 250 = 2,266 years ago. (Sometimes BC is used instead of BCE).

GASPARILLA PIRATE FESTIVAL

Every year, pirates and pirate wannabees gather in Tampa, Florida, for the Gasparilla Pirate Festival — named after a famous local pirate.

230 BCE Queen Teuta terrorises Roman and Greek ships	**220** Chinese piracy grows in the Far East	**1536** England's King Henry VIII passes laws against piracy	**1600** Spanish explorers plunder treasure in the Americas	**1650s** The first buccaneers begin their reign of terror	**1721** Maratha pirates evade capture by the British Navy	**1816** A huge fleet of ships puts an end to the Barbary corsairs	**1998** Piracy in parts of the world becomes a major problem again

1200 BCE Earliest piracy in history is recorded	**75 BCE** Julius Caesar is captured by pirates	**793** Vikings terrorise northern Europe	**1550s** Privateers serve European royalty	**1615** Barbary corsairs operate in the Mediterranean	**1678** The first Pirate Code is created	**1729** The British Navy drives pirates from their Caribbean lairs	**1883** *Treasure Island* is published	**2009** Combined Task Force 151 is formed to fight piracy

SWORD FIGHTING!

Would-be pirates — including Kate and Adam Driscoll — practise sword fighting and other skills at gatherings like Captain Redbeard's Feast in Honeyoe Lake, New York.

TWIST IT!

Cats helped control the rats and mice on board – black cats were considered especially lucky.

TARNISHED GOLDEN AGE

Over 98 per cent of buccaneers led law-abiding lives as sailors on merchant ships or in the navy before turning to a life of crime!

Pirate ships were plagued by rats, mice, lice, and fleas, and while many pirates died in battle, most died from the diseases these vermin spread onboard!

Ancient Mariners

If you were a pirate in the Middle Ages, you were made to suffer before your execution — including being dragged to your death behind a horse!

PIRATES OF THE FAR PAST

Pirating goes back to ancient Greece around 1200 BCE, when the Greeks invented the word *peiratēs*, which evolved into the word 'pirate'.

In 67 BCE, Pompey the Great gave captured pirates plots of land and helped them become farmers instead!

KEY FACTS

Roman captains often paid pirates 'wages' so they wouldn't attack their ships!

KIDNAP!

In 75 BCE, Julius Caesar was captured by pirates who demanded money for his release. Once free, Caesar returned to their lair — and had their throats cut.

TWIST IT!

The streets in the ancient town of Mykonos, Greece, were arranged in a maze pattern to foil invading pirates!

Fenrir Greyback, the werewolf in the Harry Potter books, was named after a ferocious giant wolf in ancient Viking mythology.

The pirates who captured Julius Caesar at first demanded a ransom of 20 talents of silver, but Caesar allegedly laughed and suggested he was worth at least 50!

MARAUDERS' MAYHEM

The *skogkatt*, or Norwegian Forest cat, was used by Vikings to keep their ships clear of rodents.

Ship Spoils

The Golden Age of Piracy thrived as pirates targeted the large amounts of treasure, money, and slaves being transported by ship between the Americas, Europe, and Africa.

Ripley's Explains...

TEUTA THE TERROR

Queen Teuta of Illyria terrorised the Adriatic Sea around 230 BCE. However, when more than 200 Roman ships intercepted her fleet, Teuta quickly gave up piracy!

VICIOUS VIKINGS

From 800 to 1100 AD, the Vikings ruled the northern seas, sailing their longboats in search of ships to raid.

Ripley's Believe It or Not!
In 2008, Robert McDonald built a 90-metre Viking ship from 15 million ice-cream sticks and sailed it from the Netherlands to England!

Privateers

...AND OTHER SCARY SEA DOGS

A special type of piracy known as privateering allowed certain sailors to attack foreign ships – but only if they shared the booty with their king or queen!

Privateers were still pirates at heart, however. If they were licensed to take only a certain type of vessel but couldn't find one, they would usually just attack the next ship they saw!

Although he was hanged for being a pirate, Captain Kidd was actually a privateer!

THE LINGO!

Barbary corsair
A pirate from the Barbary (North African) coast.

~

Buccaneer
A pirate of the Caribbean – named after the French word boucanier (a person who barbecues) because they cooked meat on a frame over a fire.

~

Corsair
A French pirate – the word means 'chaser'.

~

Filibuster or Fiibustier
A pirate in the 1600s, often English, Spanish, Dutch, or French.

~

Freebooter
A Dutch word for thieves in search of treasure, which was known as booty.

~

Marooner
A Spanish runaway slave or sailor.

~

Sea dog
An old or experienced sailor.

~

Sea king
A Viking pirate chief.

~

Sea rover
Another word for pirate.

BUCCANEER KING

Born in 1635, Henry Morgan was called the 'King of the Buccaneers'. King Charles II was so pleased with the piles of treasure Morgan collected for him that he made him governor of Jamaica.

WARRIORS AT SEA

England's Queen Elizabeth I gave Francis Drake permission to plunder Spanish ports and ships. In return, Drake helped her defeat the Spanish Armada fleet sent to invade England in 1588.

CRUEL CORSAIRS

When North African pirates known as Barbary corsairs captured 493 English ships between 1609 and 1625, the luckiest English sailors were sold as slaves – the unlucky ones had their throats slit.

TWIST IT!

BAD BOYS

Jean Bart, a French corsair who captured about 80 ships in the English Channel, was honoured by the King of France in 1694 – much to the frustration of the English!

Francis Drake's privateering took him far and wide – in the 1570s, he became the first Englishman to circumnavigate, or travel completely around, the world!

Jamaica's Port Royal was known as 'the most wicked and sinful city in the world', and was the favourite hideaway of Henry Morgan and other bad-to-the-bone buccaneers.

KEY FACTS

Kings and queens provided privateers with a Letter of Marque and Reprisal, which protected them from arrest if they were caught.

Pirate Ships

ALL ABOARD AND HEAVE-HO!

Ships during the Golden Age of Piracy were made of wood, and many broke apart under the strain of a heavy storm.

They were cramped, dirty, smelly places, but for many pirates, a ship was the only home they had.

Today, the world's largest cruise ship MS *Allure of the Seas* is nearly four football pitches long and 16 decks high. That's more than 90 metres longer and more than four times heavier than the *Titanic!*

KEY FACTS

Wooden ships did not have bathrooms. When pirates needed to relieve themselves, they sat on a platform called the 'beakhead bulkhead' near the front of the ship and hung their bottoms over the edge!

Crow's Nest

Rigging

Galley

Foremast

Gun Deck

Water and Beer Barrel Store

Anchor

Bilge

TWIST IT!

The poop deck is a small, raised deck in the back of the ship. When the seas got so rough that a wave broke over the stern of the ship, sailors would cry, 'Avast, we're pooped!'

Pirates arranged rat hunts to get rid of the rodents – on just one journey, a Spanish captain reported that 4,000 rats were killed!

SHIPPING OUT

Discovered in 1996 off the North Carolina shore, a 300-year-old shipwreck is believed to be none other than Blackbeard's ship, the Queen Anne's Revenge!

Main Deck

Quarter Deck

Sleeping Quarters

Poop Deck

Jolly Roger

Captain's Cabin

Food Stores

Keel

Blackbeard
Queen Anne's Revenge

~

Henry Avery
The Fancy

~

Francis Drake
The Pelican, later renamed *The Golden Hind*

~

Calico Jack
The William

~

Black Bart
Royal Fortune

~

Christopher Moody
The Rising Sun

~

William Kidd
Adventure Galley

Ripley's Explains...

Types of Sailing Ships

• **BRIGANTINE:** A large ship used by the navy or as a merchant vessel.

• **FRIGATE:** A warship (man o' war) with three masts, two decks, and as many as 90 guns.

• **GALLEON:** A large European sailing ship with three or four masts.

• **SCHOONER:** A large ship that was light, fast, and easy to sail.

• **SLOOP:** A small sailing boat with one mast.

Blackbeard

TOP PIRATE OF THE CARIBBEAN

Few pirates are as infamous as Blackbeard, who terrorised the Atlantic Ocean and Caribbean Sea from 1716 to 1718.

Probably an Englishman called Edward Teach or Thatch, Blackbeard was a privateer in the Caribbean before taking over a ship and pursuing a pirate's life.

BIG WORD ALERT

— INFAMOUS —
Well-known for being bad or doing evil things.

KEY FACTS

Blackbeard and his crew pretended to be friendly until they got close enough to attack.

Blackbeard's Jolly Roger!

When nine-year-old Beatrice Delap wrote to Captain Jack Sparrow – Johnny Depp's character in the *Pirates of the Caribbean* movies – he responded by turning up at her Greenwich, London, school in full pirate costume!

PIRATE KING

Blackbeard's crew always covered his ships' decks with sand to soak up all the blood that would be spilled in a sea battle.

Blackbeard was said to have had 14 wives. His last wife, Mary Ormond, is said to haunt the North Carolina coast, still waiting for her husband to return!

Blackbeard had no sense of honour. Legend has it he even shot members of his own crew for fun!

Pirates enjoyed a good party, and Blackbeard threw some of the best in the Caribbean. There was drinking, eating, dancing, and bonfires, and all the local pirates were invited!

TWIST IT!

A Picture of Evil

To make himself look fierce, Blackbeard carried six pistols in slings over his shoulders, shoved extra pistols down his trousers, and stuck lit matches under his hat!

Ransom

Blackbeard once captured a ship full of passengers and locked them all, including the children, in the ship's dark, dirty hold. He demanded a chest of medicine as a ransom, and it was delivered just in time to save their lives.

Missing Treasure

No one knows what Blackbeard did with his treasure – it might still be hidden somewhere!

THE PIRATE CHRONICLES

LOCAL MARAUDER

TWO CENTS
2¢ EACH

SATURDAY, OCTOBER 11, 1721

TWO CENT EDITION

NO. 11

HEADLESS HAUNTING

Facing his executioner on 20 October 1401, German pirate Klaus Störtebeker struck a last-minute deal: if his headless body managed to walk past a member of his crew, he would be freed.

According to legend, Störtebeker's corpse got up and walked past eleven of his men – before the executioner tripped him. All 70 of his crew were also beheaded, despite the deal.

THIS WEEK

PIRATES
NEEDED

~ PIRATES' WORLD OF WORK ~

Corsair Classifieds

Do you desire a life on the open sea?
Do you know your knots from your knickerbockers?
We have vacancies for keen, young, strong men who are looking for a life of adventure!

POSITIONS AVAILABLE:

- A **bosun** to organise supplies and check the ship and its sails.
- A **shipmaster** for choosing routes, navigation, and map maintenance.
- A **master gunner** to take control of all guns and ammunition.
- A **sail-maker** to oversee the stitching and care of all sails.
- A **striker** to replenish ship supplies – excellent fishing and hunting skills essential!
- A **swabbie** to wash all blood, gore, and gross body parts off the deck after battles. Must have own mop.

Applicants must have:

- *Great teamwork skills*
- *A strong stomach and sea legs*
- *No nasty diseases*

Previous experience in murder, menace, and mayhem are not necessary. We will provide all training necessary.

Minimum contract: Six months. No pension, no health benefits, no other perks – but you'll receive a daily tot of rum and all the treasure you can plunder.

Apply to: Captain D'eath, *The Marauder*, moored at Portsmouth Harbour.

WANTED: Ship's Surgeon

Carpenters or cooks with steady hands to cut off badly injured arms and legs are also strongly encouraged to apply. Must have own knives.

APPLY TO *THE SIREN*, CLEW BAY, IRELAND.

REWARD: Carpenters and other skilled labour

To join a pirate crew – either by choice or by force. If caught, they will face the death penalty, just like the other pirates.

CONTACT:
CAPTAIN B.,
THE *QUEEN ANNE'S REVENGE*,
CAROLINA,
THE NEW WORLD.

Sailor?
Try Being a Sea Dog!

Are you a navy sailor considering a life of crime? Well-known pirate captain has immediate openings for a first mate to be his second in command, and a quartermaster to guard treasure and take over in the event of his untimely demise.

APPLY IN PERSON, WITH REFERENCES, TO CAPTAIN H., *THE FURY*, MOORED IN LONDON HARBOUR.

TWIST IT!

Captured by pirates, carpenter Richard Luntly was marooned on a desert island when they overheard him planning to escape. Luntly was eventually rescued – and hanged for being a pirate anyway!

SEA-FARING FACTS

Gunpowder was carried to the cannons by younger boys in the crew known as 'powder monkeys'.

Anyone who could sing or play an instrument helped to pass the time, so pirates were always on the lookout for musicians to capture.

The Pirate Code

HOW TO BE A PIRATE: PART 1

Every pirate crew created and followed their own special set of rules called the Pirate Code, or the Articles.

First mentioned in a book called *Buccaneers of America* over 330 years ago, the Pirate Code is an important part of the story of piracy.

STEP ONE

MAKE SOME RULES

THE PIRATE CODE

1. Everyone should have a fair share of the plunder. A surgeon will receive twice as much as a carpenter.

2. Everyone should have a vote on what the crew does, where the ship goes, and who the captain will be.

3. Food and drink should be shared out equally.

4. If anyone steals from the ship's booty, he will be marooned. If he robs another pirate, he shall have his nose and ears slit before being set ashore.

5. Everyone shall keep his or her weapons clean and ready for action.

6. If anyone is injured, he or she shall be given some money. 600 pieces of eight for the loss of a right arm and 100 pieces of eight for the loss of an eye.

TWIST IT!

The Pirate Code set a strict bedtime for the pirates: candles had to be put out by 8 pm if anyone wanted to carry on partying, they had to go on deck so they didn't disturb everyone else!

CODE CLUES

To prevent his pirates from fighting aboard ship, Black Bart stated in his Code that crewmembers could not play cards for money.

**LEARN 'EM,
LIVE 'EM,
LOVE 'EM**

Anyone have any sun cream?

KEY FACTS

Red Legs Greaves had fair Scottish skin that was always sunburned. That's how he got his strange name!

SPOOKY SHIP

In 1872, the *Mary Celeste* was found in the Atlantic Ocean ten days after she set sail. Her cargo and valuables were completely untouched, but all the passengers and crewmembers had vanished!

Red Legs Greaves

Few pirates could be described as honourable, despite their Code. Red Legs Greaves, however, was a better man than most.

Originally a Scottish slave in Barbados, Red Legs was forced into piracy, became a captain, and captured both a Spanish fleet and the island of Margarita, off Venezuela.

Captured and thrown into prison, Red Legs managed to escape during an earthquake and became a pirate hunter to stay out of jail.

Unlike most pirates, Red Legs never tortured his prisoners, and he refused to rob the poor.

Sailing *the* High Seas

ALL HANDS ON DECK!*

Keeping a sailing ship afloat was a huge task that took teamwork. Sails needed to be constantly repaired, needed to be cleaned and weapons needed to be cleaned or sharpened, ready for action!

Riggers controlled the many sails on a ship. It was an incredibly dangerous job, as the ropes and wood were constantly wet with sea spray, making it easy to slip and fall into the ocean.

Caskets of rum were often called 'Nelson's blood'. When Admiral Nelson died in the Battle of Trafalgar, his body was immersed in a casket full of brandy to preserve it on the voyage back to England.

KEY FACTS

*A 'hand' is a crewmember, so this call was used in an emergency to get everyone on the deck.

THE LINGO!

Sailing a boat is a skilled job, with its own set of technical language.

Come about!
An instruction to bring a ship the full way around in the wind.

Swing the lead!
Lower a rope with a weight at the bottom, to check how deep the water is.

Heave-to!
Stop the ship! (It's not that easy to try to!)

Fly the yellow flag!
A yellow flag meant there was disease on board. Ships sometimes flew a yellow flag just to discourage pirates from attacking.

This is an instruction from a genuine guidebook for sailors, printed in 1844.

'Lift the skin up, and put into the bunt the slack of the clews (not too taut), the leech and the foot-rope, and body of the sail, being careful not to let it get forward under or hang down abaft. Then haul your bunt well up on the yard'.

A HARD LIFE

Pirate William Fly loved tying knots. At his execution, he waved at the crowd before re-tying the hangman's noose.

Although they spent their lives on the sea, many pirates couldn't swim, so falling overboard often spelled death!

Pirates didn't expect to live long lives. In fact, their average age in the 18th century was 27!

TWIST IT!

Fiji mermaids look nothing like the mythical sirens of the high seas. Instead, these man-made sideshow attractions feature the head and torso of a monkey sewn to the back half of a fish!

HO, HO, HO, ME HEARTIES!

St. Nicholas of Myra (otherwise known as Santa Claus) is the patron saint of thieves, pawnbrokers, and PIRATES!

Pirates of the East

SPINE-CHILLING SEA THIEVES

The ruthless pirates of Asia spread terror far and wide, especially across the South China Sea.

They sought power as well as treasure in this rich, thriving region.

The underwater cave system of England's Hodge Close Quarry, Cumbria, has claimed the lives of several divers, and when Peter Bardsley took this photo, he discovered a skull-shaped face was created by the reflection on the water.

Cunning Coxinga

Raiders of the Far East

From 1752 to 1832, over 200 Lanun pirate ships swarmed the merchant ships and coastal towns of Borneo, the Philippines, and New Guinea.

KEY FACTS

According to legend, Chinese pirate Cheung Po Tsai hid a vast treasure trove in a cave on Cheung Chau Island. No one has found the treasure yet!

Coxinga raised a huge army of 250,000 men and a navy of 3,000 ships to help his friend, Prince Tang, become emperor. After the emperor was defeated in battle, Coxinga turned to piracy, and successfully drove the Dutch settlers out of Taiwan (then known as Dutch Formosa) in 1661.

TWIST IT!

Lanun pirates carried huge swords that were decorated with long tresses of human hair.

Captured corsairs' ships were converted to floating prisons. Life on these diseased, rat-infested hulks was a sentence considered second only to death.

FAST FACTS

Coxinga went mad with malaria fever, and ordered his soldiers to kill his son. They refused, and Coxinga died soon after at the age of 37.

Held on the Isle of Sheppey, Kent, participants in the Annual World Plank Walking Championship are judged on their use of pirate language and costumes as well as their jumping style!

Zheng Zhilong

Chinese pirate Zheng Zhilong (1604–1661) was persuaded by the Chinese government to defend the Taiwan Strait from other pirates, and he soon became rich and powerful. Zheng's son Coxinga, however, also turned to a life of piracy and crime – and when Coxinga wouldn't surrender, his father was executed.

23

Ching Shih

THE TERROR OF THE SOUTH CHINA SEA

When Ching Shih married the pirate Cheng I, in 1801, they ransacked towns along the Chinese coastline, captured ships, and collected large hoards of treasure together.

It was just the beginning of a long pirate career for one of the world's most dangerous women.

Going Solo

When Cheng I died in 1807, his widow controlled their fleet of 300 ships and up to 40,000 pirates, including men, women, and children.

Smart Tactics

Instead of attacking local villagers, Ching Shih made sure they were paid for any rice and wine the pirates consumed.

The Cruel Queen of the Sea

Ching Shih used cruelty to keep her pirate crew in line – including cutting off pirates' ears, flogging them, nailing their feet to the deck of a ship, or throwing them overboard!

SHE-DEVIL OF THE SEA

Pirate captains who worked for Ching Shih often gave themselves scary or strange names, such as 'Scourge of the Eastern Sea', 'Frog's Meal', and 'Jewel of the Whole Crew'.

Ching Shih didn't consider herself a smuggler, and preferred to say she 'transshipped goods' instead.

The Chinese government offered to let Ching Shih go free if she promised to give up pirating, which she did. She died of old age in 1844.

TWIST IT!

Keeping It in the Family

Cheung Po Tsai, a fisherman's son, was kidnapped and adopted by Cheng I and Ching Shih. According to legend, when Cheng I died, Cheung Po married his adoptive mother, and together they carried on the family business of piracy.

STINKPOT

Chinese pirates were infamous for their creation of the stinkpot. Filled with gunpowder and sulphur, stinkpots were thrown onto the deck of their victims' ship, where they released such a foul smell most sailors would jump overboard to avoid it!

KEY FACTS

The first rule in Ching Shih's Pirate Code was that anyone who disobeyed her would be beheaded on the spot!

MERMAID SCULPTURE

BIG WORD ALERT

SMUGGLER

A person who moves goods in and out of the country, against the laws of the land.

Ripley's Believe It or Not!®

Greg Lewis of Chesterfield, Virginia, created this mermaid sculpture from 67,000 toothpicks!

Flying *the* Jolly Roger

HOW TO BE A PIRATE: PART 2

Imagine you are a sailor who has decided to turn to a life of crime. You've staged a mutiny, thrown your annoying captain overboard, and persuaded your crewmates to join you in a new life of maritime mugging.

Now, you need to choose a flag, dress like a pirate, and practice speaking like an old sea dog.

STEP ONE — CHOOSE YOUR FLAG

▶ A red skeleton on the front of the flag.

Edward Low

Some believe the French name 'Jolie Rouge' (pretty red) gave us the name 'Jolly Roger' for a pirate's flag. You'll need to design your own flag, just as the pirates of old did. Here are some samples to help:

Christopher Moody

Walter Kennedy

▶ A red flag (!), a golden winged hourglass, a white arm holding a dagger, and a golden skull and crossbones all in a row.

Edward England

◀ The typical skull and crossbones, along with a figure holding a sword and an hourglass.

Christopher Condent

◀ The classic skull and crossbones design, with the crossbones below the skull.

◀ A long black banner with three of the classic skull and crossbones in a row.

You'll need to look menacing, brutal, and swashbuckling. As the captain, you can go overboard (not literally!) on your fashion statement, with flouncy fabrics and lots of flashy jewellery.

Need supplies for your pirate crew? San Francisco's 826 Valencia Pirate Supply Store and website offer everything from captain's logs to mermaid bait!

PIRATE PETS

Cats, monkeys, and even lizards were popular pets aboard ship. To pirates in Madagascar, the panther chameleon must have seemed like a mythical monster with independently roving eyes. This predator's lightning-fast, insect-snatching tongue can extend nearly the length of its body!

Who's a pretty boy then?

Will I need a parrot?

Definitely. Parrots are super intelligent, and can learn to mimic things you say. Once you catch one in a tropical forest, you can sell it for lots of money when you sail to Europe or North America.

Ripley's Explains...

BIG WORD ALERT

— MUTINY —

When a crew disobeys the captain and takes control of their ship.

THE LINGO!

You'll need to learn how to speak like a pirate, so here are some useful phrases:

Aye-aye!
A pirate's way of saying 'yes', 'OK', or 'I'll get right on it!'

~

Aaargh!
A deep growling sound that makes every pirate seem even scarier.

~

You filthy bilge rat!
The 'bilge' was the lowest part of the ship, so it was dark, dank, and smelly. Calling someone a bilge rat was a terrible insult.

~

Shiver me timbers!
The 'timbers' were the masts, and they might shake if struck by a cannonball. The phrase means 'What a surprise!'

~

Avast ye, me swashbuckler mates!
'Avast ye' means 'Hey, stop that!' It came from a Dutch phrase used to tell sailors to stop pulling the ropes. 'Swashbuckler' is a term used to describe a daring adventurer, including a pirate.

TEMPORARY TATTOOS

TREASURE BURIAL SAND

SCURVY BEGONE

DYSENTERY

PINK EYE

GANGRENE

BLACKWATER FEVER

MERMAID BAIT or REPELLENT

Pirates on Parade

'Calico' Jack Rackham's Jolly Roger was a skull above crossed swords.

CHIC, NOT CHEAP!

Pirates often dressed flamboyantly in fine clothes for special occasions and when they went on land.

They adopted a more relaxed look for everyday work, wearing a uniform that was practical for sailing a ship or fighting.

NO SKIRTS? NO PROBLEM!

While in Nassau, Bahamas, Rackham fell in love with a sailor's wife named Anne Bonny. She and another woman named Mary Read joined Rackham's pirate crew. Women pirates often dressed as men, as men's clothes were far more practical for life aboard a ship than a woman's corsets and long skirts.

'Calico' Jack Rackham

Mary Read dressed as a man long before she became a pirate to make it easier to find a job.

Captain 'Calico' Jack Rackham, a British sailor who turned pirate in 1718, became famous for his fancy outfits – the word 'calico' is used to describe fabrics that are printed with colourful, flowery patterns as well as plain, cream – coloured cottons.

Ripley's Believe It or Not!®

A genetic mutation has given Whipper, a parakeet in New Zealand, fancy feathers to grace any dandy pirate's shoulders!

PATCH SWITCH

Many pirates wore a patch over one eye to keep it adapted to the light outside. If a battle broke out and a pirate had to shimmy below, he would cover his 'outdoor' eye with the patch, allowing him to see better in the dark.

Eye-eye, Cap'n!

KEY FACTS

Pirates often wore gold hoop earrings because it was believed they helped reduce seasickness.

The unique stripe over this insect's eye gives the impression of an eye patch, so the scientists who discovered it in 2013 named it the pirate ant!

Tri-cornered hats were often made of leather so they weren't ruined by salty sea spray.

A pirate's clothes might not fit very well if he had stolen them.

A fine silk necktie or bandana was useful to catch sweat as it poured off the pirate's head.

Woollen or canvas shirts and trousers were warm and sturdy. Trousers often ended at the knee (breeches) or above the ankle.

Jackets were often blue, waistcoats were red, and shirts were often checked.

Clothes needed to be short but tight fitting so they didn't get caught on the rigging.

Belts were often worn across the shoulder – they were too heavy for the waist when laden with pistols.

Pirates and sailors usually went barefoot at sea. This made climbing the ropes easier.

Cutlass, Pistol and Cannon

PIRATE WEAPONRY

Pirates chose from a large armoury of weapons during a mission to plunder, smash, and grab.

The type and variety of weapons differed across the world – and through the centuries.

Treasury Street in St. Augustine, Florida, is the narrowest street in the United States. It was purposely built to be 2 metres wide – just enough room for two men to carry a chest of gold to the Royal Spanish Treasury from ships docked on the bay, but not wide enough for a horse and carriage to drive by and snatch the loot!

BAY ST.

AUGUSTINE, Fla. Treasury Street, the Narrowest Street in the U.S.

TWIST IT!

Guns were named after the weight of the iron round shot they fired. 'Four-pounders' were the most common size, while smaller grape shot was used to hit sailors on deck without causing damage to the ship.

Except for warning shots, pirates avoided firing their guns. Their goal was to rob and steal ships, not destroy them!

Captain Kidd's 34-gun warship, *Adventure Galley*, lost its final battle not to the navy, but to shipworms – pesky underwater molluscs that love to munch on wood!

BANG, BANG, BOOM!

Ripley's Explains...

Gunpowder

This is a fine powder explosive that was invented in China and was used in early guns and cannons – and it makes fireworks explode. Pirates used lots of gunpowder, but they had to keep it dry or it wouldn't work.

Granado

Pirates threw granado shells, which were an early type of hand grenade, a small bomb that is thrown at the enemy. The word 'granado' came from *granada*, the Spanish word for pomegranate.

Flintlock Pistol

A noisy gun that is fired by a spark created from a flint.

WEAPONRY

Cutlass

A short sword, often curved.

Thumbs up:
Guns can kill lots of people quite quickly.

Thumbs down:
If pistols get damp – which they often do at sea – they don't work. They are difficult to aim, too.

Thumbs up:
Great for fighting in cramped spaces and for slashing ropes.

Thumbs down:
Hard work to kill people, and you can only kill one person at a time.

Scimitar

A heavy, curved sword commonly used by Muslims and Indian pirates.

Axe

A sharp blade and a hammer on one wooden handle.

Fire Bomb

Anything that can be thrown at a wooden ship to set it on fire.

Thumbs up:
This sword can slice and slash, so it does a lot of damage.

Thumbs down:
It is heavy and more difficult to control than European cutlasses.

Thumbs up:
Great for attacking people, smashing open doors, cutting ropes and digging out fire bombs from a ship's timbers.

Thumbs down:
Heavy, so it needs a pirate with big muscles to use it.

Thumbs up:
Tar bombs are easy to make using a rope dipped in a burning lump of tar.

Thumbs down:
You need to be close enough to the enemy ship to throw it on board.

Thumbs up:
A perfect weapon for knocking down sails and masts, bombing a town from the sea, or putting a hole in the side of a ship.

Thumbs down:
Heavy, expensive, and hard to reload.

Cannon

A huge, heavy gun that fires cannonballs.

Black Bart

WICKED, BUT BRAVE

In just four years, Bartholomew Roberts, or Black Bart, captured more than 400 ships and terrorised the Caribbean and North American coasts.

He and his pirate crew were so powerful they almost put an end to all trade between Europe and the Americas!

Reign of Terror

From 1720 to 1721, Black Bart attacked English, Dutch, French, and Spanish ships around the Caribbean and along the eastern coast to Newfoundland in Canada.

From Sailor to Slave

Born in Wales in 1682, Roberts joined the British Navy. Enslaved when pirates captured his ship, he soon earned his freedom and rose to the rank of captain.

A Cutthroat Killer

In just one action, Bart ambushed 14 French ships, torturing and killing the sailors aboard. He took over a huge brigantine that he named Good Fortune to celebrate his success.

Bart Meets His End

Bart eventually sailed to Africa, where a pirate hunter named Chaloner Ogle fired at his flagship. When the smoke from their battle cleared, Black Bart was found slumped dead over a cannon.

SKULL AND CROSS-BULB

Black Bart's Jolly Roger was a drawing of himself holding an hourglass with a skeleton!

Ripley's Believe It or Not!®

Dutch artist Hans van Bentem makes beautiful crystal chandeliers in the most unique and unusual designs—including this stunning skull and crossbones chandelier, which took about two months to create and is worth more than £10,500!

SCHOOL AND CROSSBONES

Ripley's Believe It or Not!®

Dale Price of American Fork, Utah, has waved his teenage son Rain off to high school every morning wearing over 170 different costumes. He received thunderous applause from the entire school bus for his pirate garb, complete with a peg leg!

BART'S BOTTOM LINE

Although he did terrible things, Black Bart didn't approve of drinking alcohol or swearing!

Black Bart once burned a ship knowing there were 80 slaves aboard and that they would all die.

Black Bart's death in 1722 marked the beginning of the end of the Golden Age of Piracy.

Black Bart Roberts lives on in popular culture. In the movie *The Princess Bride*, the character Dread Pirate Roberts was named in honour of him!

TWIST IT!

33

Pillage _and_ Plunder

HOW TO BE A PIRATE: PART 3

Successful pirates have a few tricks up their sleeves when it comes to catching a ship.

Follow these top tips to become a fearsome, plundering pirate and ruthless scallywag.

Sneaky Thieves

On a summer's night in 1720, 'Calico' Jack Rackham, Anne Bonny, Mary Read, and a few members of their pirate crew rowed across Nassau Harbor in the Bahamas. Silently, they climbed aboard a British sloop called The William and sailed it away!

Anne Bonny

TWIST IT!

Anne Bonny was said to have a fierce temper. Before she became a pirate, she once became so angry that she stabbed her maid to death.

BAD ATTITUDE

Pirates of the 16th century proved they were 'macho' by drinking a mixture of rum and gunpowder!

ALL ABOARD!

Once a pirate crew got close to their target, there was no time to lose. The first task was to send the ship's captain over to their pirate ship in a small boat. He would be kept hostage there while the pirates ransacked his vessel.

DEADLY BATTLES

If there was a battle, the air would become thick with gunpowder smoke and the sound of blades clashing as sailors and pirates fought hand-to-hand.

BIG WORD ALERT

— PILLAGE & PLUNDER —

Both of these words mean stealing while using violence at the same time.

Pirates didn't have a bank or cash machine onboard, so some made a secret stash to hide their cash.

Ripley's Explains...

How to Capture a Ship

Many ships during the Golden Age of Piracy were equipped with rows of cannons, and plundering pirates put them to good use. A common tactic was to sail alongside (broadside) the enemy and blast them with all their cannons – perhaps as many as ten cannons firing at once – while the men fired with muskets and pistols at very close range.

CAVE-INGS ACCOUNT

The cave through Dungeon Rock in Lynn, Massachusetts, was dug in 1852 by Hiram Marble, who believed the ghost of pirate Thomas Veale was directing him to his treasure. Marble dug until his death, but he never found the loot.

STEP TWO

WORK HARD, PLAY HARDER!

Believe It or Not!®

Redemption Part I by artist Peter Riss is a children's jungle gym on display at Heilig-Kreuz Church in Munich, Germany – in their former cemetery!

SKELETONS OF FUN!

KEY FACTS

Pirates did not make their prisoners walk the plank. That's a popular myth!

Pirate Treasure

It is difficult to say exactly what a pirate's treasure trove might be worth today.

However, there is no doubt that a life of crime did pay – unless the hangman got them before they had a chance to spend all their gold!

According to legend, when a pirate buried treasure, he would kill someone and bury his or her body on top of it. This way, the murdered person's ghost would protect the booty!

TREASURE MAPS

Historians aren't sure if pirates really buried their treasure on islands, recording the location with an X on a map. In fact, the idea seems to have come from Robert Louis Stevenson's famous novel, *Treasure Island*, published in 1883.

X marks the spot!

Ripley's Explains...

Precious Swag

If you found a casket full of doubloons, ducats, and pieces of eight, would you be happy – or confused?

Ripley explains the perplexing subject of old currencies:

Reale = a small silver Spanish coin
Piece of Eight = a coin worth 8 reales
Dollar/Peso = alternative names for a piece of eight
Escudo = a coin worth 2 pieces of eight
Doubloon = a gold coin worth 4 pieces of eight
Ducats = gold and silver coins used in the Mediterranean region

Today, a piece of eight is worth about £50!

Florida's Annual Lower Keys Underwater Music Festival combines a pirate's love for music and the sea. Hundreds dive 9 metres beneath the waves to hear musicians play on the ocean floor.

This ancient chest was once used to store pirate booty – and Robert Ripley himself stored some of his most valuable treasures in it!

LOVELY LOOT!

Pirates didn't just want gold. They needed everyday items, too.

~

Cloth such as silk, canvas, and cotton

Maps and charts

Navigational equipment

Medicine

Weapons

Tobacco for their pipes

Anchor chains

Cattle, chicken, fish

Ropes

Spare sails

Carpentry tools

Sugar

Wine and rum

TWIST IT!

In 2015, while studying a shipwreck off the coast of Madagascar that is thought to be the pirate ship Adventure Galley, archaeologists discovered a 50-kilogram slab of silver that may have belonged to Captain Kidd!

TREASURE TALES

While every pirate dreamed of treasure chests filled with gold and jewels, sugar and tobacco shipped from the Americas to Europe were also popular booty – they could be sold for a king's ransom.

BIG WORD ALERT

CURRENCY

The coins and notes used as money in a country.

KEY FACTS

Pieces of eight were used as currency in the United States until 1857.

Pirate Hunters

Governments hired pirate hunters to give the sea robbers a taste of their own medicine.

One of them, British Navy Lieutenant Robert Maynard, is most famous for capturing the notorious Captain Blackbeard at Ocracoke Island in North Carolina.

Blackbeard's Death

One of Maynard's ships was badly damaged after Blackbeard bombarded it with cannon fire. The pirates clambered on board, not realizing Maynard's crew were hiding below with their pistols ready, and were slaughtered.

Maynard shot Blackbeard, who still had the strength to raise his cutlass – before a sailor slashed his throat. After the battle, Blackbeard's head was hung from the bow of Maynard's sloop as a gruesome warning to other pirates.

SHORT ROPE, LONG DANCE

Using a short rope ensured that hanging victims would die by strangulation, slowly turning purple as they 'danced the hempen jig'.

Pirates who made the Bahamas their hideout would feast on the wild boar they found — and now, a 115-kilogram wild boar named Babe lives there in luxury with the only two humans who reside on a private island. Babe feasts on hot dogs, apples, pasta, and the occasional beer!

PARDON THE PIRATES

Privateer Woodes Rogers (1679–1732) was made governor of the Bahamas and told to destroy the pirate fleets around the islands. He first offered them amnesty, which meant the king would pardon their misdeeds. Eager to avoid a date with the gallows, almost 300 pirates turned in their swords!

THE GENTLEMAN PIRATE

Stede Bonnet was a wealthy Barbados landowner who met Blackbeard, and was so impressed with his tales of adventure that he decided to become a buccaneer himself. After a long and bloody fight with a pirate hunter, Bonnet surrendered, but managed to escape!

TWIST IT!

In 1696, Captain Kidd was hired to be a pirate hunter, but became a pirate himself. During his execution the rope broke, so he had to be hanged twice!

Pirates rarely betrayed one another, but Cyril Hood offered to tell pirate hunters where to find buccaneer Abraham Cooke in exchange for just a single bottle of rum!

HUNTER TURNED HUNTED

Stede Bonnet was pardoned in 1718 and became a privateer. However, he decided that he preferred being a pirate and returned to his life of crime!

They Got Away...

...AND LIVED TO TELL THE TALE!

A few lucky pirates managed to escape capture and retired to enjoy a quiet life spending their vast amounts of treasure.

Some were even honoured by their governments and given important jobs!

MARY KILL-THE-CREW

Lady Mary Killigrew (1530–1580) had everyone aboard a Spanish ship murdered while she plundered two barrels full of pieces of eight. Her pirate crew were captured and sentenced to hang, but Queen Elizabeth I took pity on her, and she served a short jail sentence instead.

Ripley's Explains...

SECRETS OF SUCCESS

Many pirates got away with a life of crime because they shared their booty with powerful people who turned a blind eye to the evil events off the coast. Even pirate hunters could be bribed this way.

Avery's Jolly Roger is recorded as having the same skull and crossbones design on both a red or black background.

AN UNSURE END

Known as the 'King of Pirates,' Captain Henry Avery attacked the Ganj-i-Sawai, a huge ship laden with treasure, in 1695. No one knows what happened to Avery afterward — some people said he retired to a life of great luxury on a tropical island, while others claimed he lost all his money and died in poverty in England.

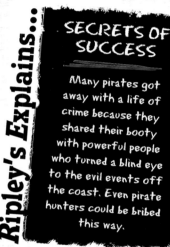

Ripley's Believe It or Not!

This model of Captain Jack Sparrow, created by Thailand-based company Art From Steel, measures over 2 metres high, weighs several hundred kilograms, and is made completely of recycled car parts!

TWIST IT!

Barbarossa – also known as Redbeard – was one of the most feared corsairs in the 16th century. The ruthless pirate was so unafraid of ever being punished, he wrote and published his memoirs when he retired, confessing to everything!

When captured after plundering a Spanish treasure ship, pirate Bartolomeu Portugues jumped overboard and escaped, using pottery jars he'd stolen from the hold as buoys to stay afloat until he reached shore.

Privateer Francis Drake ransacked Spanish colonies and plundered merchant ships. When he was knighted for his efforts by Queen Elizabeth I, the Spanish king was furious!

ESCAPE

When Jack, the Capuchin monkey who stars in the *Pirates of the Caribbean* films, arrived in Queensland to begin filming the sequel, *Pirates of the Caribbean: Dead Men Tell No Tales,* both he and his primate understudy were placed in 30-day pest quarantine in accordance with the law Down Under!

The Black Spot

...AND OTHER GRUESOME ENDS

A captured pirate usually faced a brief trial, followed by hanging.

However, a pirate who betrayed his own crew, or disobeyed the Pirate Code, could face a far worse fate!

THE BLACK SPOT

In the novel *Treasure Island*, pirates considered traitors to their ship were given a 'black spot' on a piece of paper... and a death sentence.

Pirates in Jamaica were put in a narrow metal cage called a gibbet and hung in the sun. They would die a slow and painful death from the burning heat.

Brutal Buccaneers

Buccaneers and other pirates had a nasty array of punishments they used against traitors, unpopular captains, and any poor prisoners they captured.

Keel hauling

The unfortunate victim was tied to a rope and dragged the length of the boat along the keel, from front to back. Apart from the high chance of drowning, his body would be ripped to shreds by the many rough shellfish attached to the keel.

Marooning

Prisoners and pirates were sometimes simply left on a deserted island, perhaps with a bottle of rum for company.

Cat-o'-nine-tails

This was a whip with nine leather strips that were knotted with pieces of metal at the end. A severe whipping with one of these instruments of torture could be enough to kill a person.

This customised pirate bedroom in Minnesota features a rope bridge, a steering wheel, and a slide from the ship-shaped bed. There is even a small jail cell for mutiny-minded brothers and sisters!

THE LINGO!

Blow the Man Down
This was a popular sea shanty, or song. It means, 'knock a man to the ground'.

~

Feed the Fish
If a pirate was thrown overboard, he would become food for the fish.

~

Sharkbait
If a pirate was told he was 'sharkbait', he knew he was about to be thrown overboard.

~

Davy Jones's Locker
This is the pirate's term for the bottom of the sea – so a pirate who was going to Davy Jones's Locker was about to die. No one knows who Davy Jones really was!

GRUESOME FATES

One evil pirate made a ship's captain cut off his own ears and eat them.

When a captured sailor once complained about his treatment aboard a pirate ship, the pirate captain took a needle and thread and sewed up his mouth!

TWIST IT!

NO FOND FAREWELLS

Sea robbers often attacked coastal towns and villages, and put the lives of honest sailors in danger. It's no wonder that when a pirate was caught, he was often executed while being jeered and spat at by onlookers.

Pirates *in* Today's World

MODERN PIRATES, MYTHS AND LEGENDS

Many myths and legends have arisen around piracy in the past. However, some cutthroat criminals still operate today, both at sea and at home.

DANGER AT SEA

Modern Somali pirates attack cargo ships or tankers carrying valuable loads of oil. Often they simply steal the crew's belongings and cargo, but sometimes they hold the ship for ransom – or worse.

SPEARS AS AMMO

Tra-la-la!

Ripley's Believe It or Not!

Songs by pop star Britney Spears are blasted by British naval officers in an attempt to scare off pirates along the east coast of Africa!

DIGITAL PIRACY

Stealing digital media is illegal – always check that you have permission to swap downloaded music with friends, rip CDs, or share software, or you might find yourself being accused of being an Internet pirate!

PIRATIN' APP

People using pirated versions of the Today Calendar Pro app virtually walk the plank! A 'Walk the Plank' event appears onscreen with the message, 'That's what ye get fer piratin' matey!'

TWIST IT!

The modern-day pirate hunters in Combined Task Force 151 use high-tech warships and equipment to combat today's tech-savvy buccaneers.

The concentrated sound attacker's hearing from over 275 metres away. — the concentrated sound can permanently affect the

PIRATE TECH 101

Unlike pirates of old, modern pirates usually operate from shore, and may use speedboats to reach their targets. Cruise ships are attractive targets for today's pirates. They defend themselves by blasting sonic cannons

KEY FACT

As many as 400 ships are attacked by pirates every year, mainly around Indonesia, Panama, Somalia, and Bangladesh.

POP CULTURE PIRATES

Sao Feng, a character in *Pirates of the Caribbean: At the World's End*, is based on the 18th-century Chinese pirate Cheung Po Tsai.

The fictional character Captain Jack Sparrow is believed to be based in part on another fictional pirate – Long John Silver, a trickster in *Treasure Island*.

INDEX

Bold numbers refer to main entries; numbers in *italic* refer to the illustrations.

ACKNOWLEDGEMENTS

Cover Illustrations by John Graziano; **2** (c) Illustration by John Graziano, (t) © XiaImages—iStock.com; **2–3** (bgd) © XiaImages—iStock.com, © daksun—Shutterstock.com, © photocell—Shutterstock.com, (t) © sharpner—Shutterstock.com; **3** (t) © mj007—Shutterstock.com, (b) Illustration by John Graziano; **4** (b) Illustration by John Graziano; **4–5** (bgd) © Fedor Selivanov—Shutterstock.com; **5** (c) Illustration by John Graziano; **6** © 1971yes—iStock.com; **7** (t/r) © ZUMA Press, Inc./Alamy, (t/l) © Dennis MacDonald/Alamy, (b) Lorie (O'Donnell) Finger; **8** (t) *William Marsh being dragged to his execution in 1240* (vellum), Paris, Matthew (c.1200-59)/Private Collection/ Peter Newark Pictures/Bridgeman Images, (b/r) Illustration by John Graziano; **9** (t/l) © Jan Faukner—Shutterstock.com, (t/r) Illustration by John Graziano, (b) © WENN; **10** (b/l) Illustration by John Graziano, (b/r) © Seregam—Shutterstock.com; **10–11** (bgd) © Jozef Sowa—Shutterstock.com, © Fedor Selivanov—Shutterstock.com, © Picsfive—Shutterstock.com; **11** (t/r) Photo by Mohammed Talatene/ Anadolu Agency/Getty Images, (b/r) © peachroomtom—iStock.com; **12** (t) © User: Jorge in Brazil/Wikimedia Commons/CC-BY-SA-3.0; **12–13** (b) Illustrations by John Graziano; **13** (t/l) Courtesy of a private collector, (t/r) © PlanForYou—Shutterstock.com, (r) © Seregam— Shutterstock.com; **14** Illustration by John Graziano; **14–15** (bgd) © www.BillionPhotos.com—Shutterstock.com; **15** (t/r) Illustrations by John Graziano, (c/r) Richard Young/Rex/REX USA, (b/l) Zubova Zhanna; **16** (c) P.PLAILLY/E.DAYNES/SCIENCE SOURCE; **16–17** (b) © JDawnInk—Getty Images; **17** (b) © kontur-vid—Shutterstock.com; **18** © SuriyaPhoto—Shutterstock.com; **19** (t) Photo by David L Ryan/The Boston Globe via Getty Images, (c) Brigantine *Mary Celeste*, commanded by Benjamin Briggs, found without crew, drifting towards Strait of Gibraltar in 1872, print, 19th century/De Agostini Picture Library/Bridgeman Images, (b) Illustration by John Graziano; **20** (c) © Shutterwolf—iStock.com, (b) © Peter Lange/Laird McGillicuddy; **20–21** (bgd) © Jose Angel Astor Rocha—Shutterstock. com; **21** (t) © Seregam—Shutterstock.com, (b) © Signed model release filed with Shutterstock, Inc—Shutterstock.com, (r) Courtesy of Juan Cabana; **22** (t) © Andrew Price/Rex/REX USA, (b) Illustration by John Graziano; **23** (t) © Elite Home Theater Seating/Rex/REX USA, (b/l) Illustration by John Graziano, (b/r) © Eddie Mulholland/Rex/REX USA; **24** (t) *Madame Ching, legendary Chinese Pirate Queen* (engraving), American School, (18th century)/Private Collection/Peter Newark Historical Pictures/Bridgeman Images, (b) Illustration by John Graziano; **24–25** (bgd) © kanate—Shutterstock.com, © Picsfive—Shutterstock.com; **25** (c) Illustration by John Graziano; **26** Illustration by John Graziano; **27** (t, t/l, c, c/l, b/l) 826 Valencia, 826valencia.org/store, (t/r) © Chris Mattison/FLPA/Science Source, (c/r) Illustration by John Graziano, (r) © Seregam—Shutterstock.com; **28** (t) Illustration by John Graziano, (c) *Mary Read, female pirate* (coloured engraving), American School, (19th century)/Private Collection /Peter Newark Historical Picture/Bridgeman Images, (b) Illustrations by John Graziano; **29** (t) © REX USA, (c/l) © Scott Rothstein—Shutterstock.com, (c/r) © SchubPhoto—Shutterstock.com, (b) Dr. Roland Schultz, (r) © Landysh—Shutterstock.com; **30** (b/c) © Fablok—Shutterstock.com, (b/r) Illustration by John Graziano; **30–31** (bgd) © Peshkova—Shutterstock .com; **31** (bgd) © Xial Images, © daksun—Shutterstock.com, (t/l) © mj007—Shutterstock.com, (t/r) © andrewburgess—iStock.com, (c/l) © XiaImages—iStock.com, (c/r) Illustration by John Graziano, (b/l) © sharpner—Shutterstock.com, (b/r) Illustration by John Graziano; **32** (t, b) Illustrations by John Graziano; **32–33** (bgd) © Picsfive—Shutterstock.com; **33** (t) PHOTOGRAPHY BY GAVIN BERNARD/ BARCROFT MEDIA LTD, (c) © Price Family/Rex/REX USA, (b) Illustration by John Graziano; **34** (c) Illustration by John Graziano, (b) © Harry H Marsh—Shutterstock.com; **35** (t) © Melkor3D—Shutterstock.com, (c) By Ehkastning (Own work) [CC BY-SA 3.0 (http://creativecommons.org/licenses/by-sa/3.0)], via Wikimedia Commons, (b/l) © Peter Riss, (b/r) © joshblake— iStock.com; **36** (c/l) © topshotUK—iStock.com, (c/r) Mary Evans Picture Library, (b) © JOE CICAK—iStock.com; **36–37** (bgd) © val lawless—Shutterstock.com; **37** (t/l) BILL KEOUGH/AFP/Getty Images, (t/r) © Seregam—Shutterstock.com, (b/r) © thanakritphoto— Shutterstock.com; **38** (l) *The Capture of the Pirate Blackbeard, 1718*, Ferris, Jean Leon Gerome (1863-1930)/Private Collection/ Bridgeman Images, (b/r) © Maksim Shmeljov—Shutterstock.com; **38–39** (bgd) © theromb—Shutterstock.com; **39** (t/l) Public domain, via Wikimedia Commons, (t/r) © Gary Roberts/REX USA; **40** Illustrations by John Graziano; **40–41** (bgd) © Phiseksit— Shutterstock.com, © Eky Studio—Shutterstock.com; **41** (l) Sculpture by Art of Steel/Photo courtesy of Steve Campbell, (t/r) *Queen Elizabeth I knighting Francis Drake*, Matania, Fortunino (1881-1963)/Private Collection/© Look and Learn/Bridgeman Images, (c/r) Illustration by John Graziano, (b/r) Photo by Steve Granitz/WireImage/Getty; **42** (l) © Apriori1—iStock.com, (b) © timhughes—iStock. com; **43** (t/l) © Seregam—Shutterstock.com, (t/r) © Rex/REX USA, (b) *Dead men tell no tales*, 1899 (oil on canvas en grisaille), Pyle, Howard (1853-1911)/© American Illustrators Gallery, NYC/www.asapworldwide.com/Bridgeman Images; **44** (t) Photo by Jonas Gratzer/LightRocket via Getty Images, (c) © Featureflash—Shutterstock.com, (b) © pushlama—iStock.com; **45** (t/l) Today Calendar for Android/Developer: Jack Underwood/Visual Design: Liam Spradlin, (t/r) © jiawangkun—Shutterstock.com, (b/l) AFP/Getty Images, (b/r) Mary Evans Picture Library

Key: t = top, b = bottom, c = center, l = left, r = right, sp = single page, bgd = background

All other photos are from Ripley Entertainment Inc.

Every attempt has been made to acknowledge correctly and contact copyright holders, and we apologize in advance for any unintentional errors or omissions, which will be corrected in future editions.